Money Math with Sebastian Pig and Friends
At the Farmer's Market

eries Math Consultant:
ssi Heppelmann
ementary School Teacher
rmington School District
innesota

eries Literacy Consultant:
llan A. De Fina, Ph.D.
ean, College of Education / Professor of Literacy Education
ew Jersey City University
st President of the New Jersey Reading Association

By Jill Anderson

Illustrated by Amy Huntington

Enslow Elementary
an imprint of

Enslow Publishers, Inc.
40 Industrial Road
Box 398
Berkeley Heights, NJ 07922
USA

http://www.enslow.com

To Parents and Teachers:

As you read Sebastian's story with a child,

*Rely on the pictures to see the math visually represented.

*Use Sebastian's notebook, which summarizes the math at hand.

*Practice money math with your child using the activites on page 30.

Enslow Elementary, an imprint of Enslow Publishers, Inc.

Enslow Elementary® is a registered trademark of Enslow Publishers, Inc.

Copyright © 2009 by Enslow Publishers, Inc.

Library of Congress Cataloging-in-Publication Data
Anderson, Jill, 1968-
  Money math with Sebastian pig and friends : at the farmer's market / written by Jill Anderson ; illustrated by Amy Huntington.
       p. cm. — (Math fun with Sebastian pig and friends!)
  Includes bibliographical references and index.
  Summary: "A fun and simple review of basic money math for beginning students"—Provided by publisher.
  ISBN-13: 978-0-7660-3364-1
  ISBN-10: 0-7660-3364-3
  1. Counting—Juvenile literature. 2. Coins, American—Juvenile literature.
3. Money—Juvenile literature. 4. Mathematics—Study and teaching (Elementary)—Juvenile literature. I. Huntington, Amy, ill. II. Title.
  QA113.A5654 2009
  513.2'11—dc22
                        2008028476

Editorial Direction: Red Line Editorial, Inc.

Printed in the United States of America

10 9 8 7 6 5 4 3 2 1

Table of Contents

Sebastian Pig and Louie are going shopping at the farmer's market. Can you help them? Count their coins. How much money do they have? Then help Sebastian figure out how to pay. Keep track of how much money is left. Need a hint? Look in Sebastian's notebook.

Packing for a Picnic

It's a beautiful day! Sebastian and Louie are packing a picnic lunch.

Sebastian looks inside the cooler. He is not sure there is enough to eat.

"Let's buy more food at the farmer's market," Sebastian says.

How much money do the friends have? They look in their pockets.

How Many Pennies?

First they count their pennies. Sebastian has two pennies.
Louie has three. How much is that? Each penny is worth one
cent. So Sebastian counts by ones. He writes the amount in
his notebook.

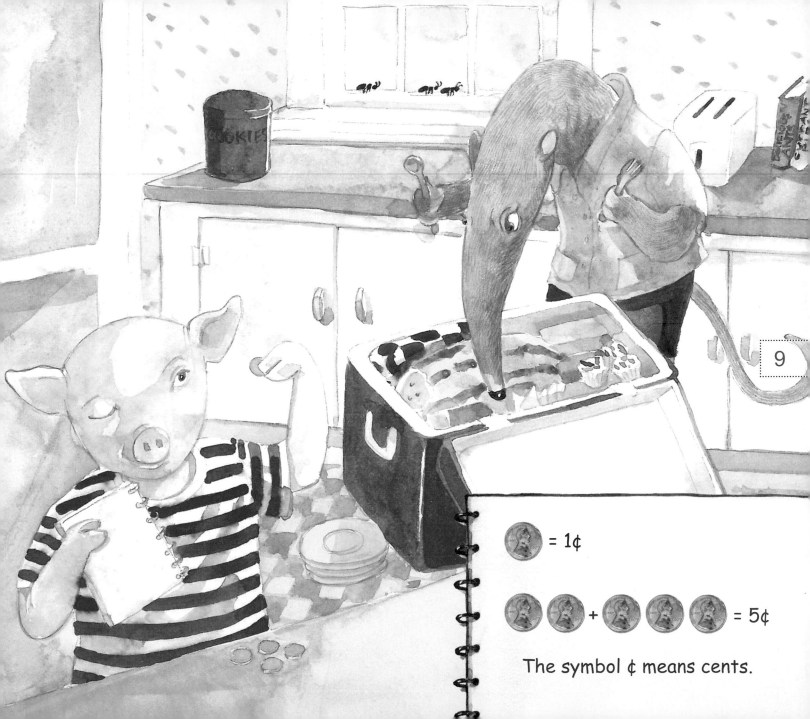

9

 = 1¢

  +   = 5¢

The symbol ¢ means cents.

Nickel Know-How

Next they count their nickels. Sebastian has four nickels. Louie has zero nickels. Each nickel is worth five cents. Sebastian counts by fives. How much do they have?

= 5¢

= 20¢

12

 = 10¢

 +     = 50¢

Time to Count Dimes

They still do not have enough money for shopping. They need coins that are worth more. Dimes are more like it! Sebastian has one, and Louie has four. Each dime is worth 10 cents. Louie helps Sebastian count by tens.

The Quarter Count

Do they have any quarters? There's one. It is worth 25 cents.

15

= 25¢

One Dollar

How much do all of these coins add up to? Sebastian counts the money. He starts with the quarter. He works his way down to the pennies. Sebastian and Louie have one dollar to spend.

100¢ = $1.00

Time to Shop!

The friends go to the farmer's market. Sebastian likes carrots. One bunch costs 25¢. He gives the farmer the quarter. How much money is left?

100¢ - 25¢ = 75¢

A Chunk of Cheese

Louie likes cheese. Sebastian picks out some cheese for his friend. He takes out a dime and a nickel. They add up to 15¢.

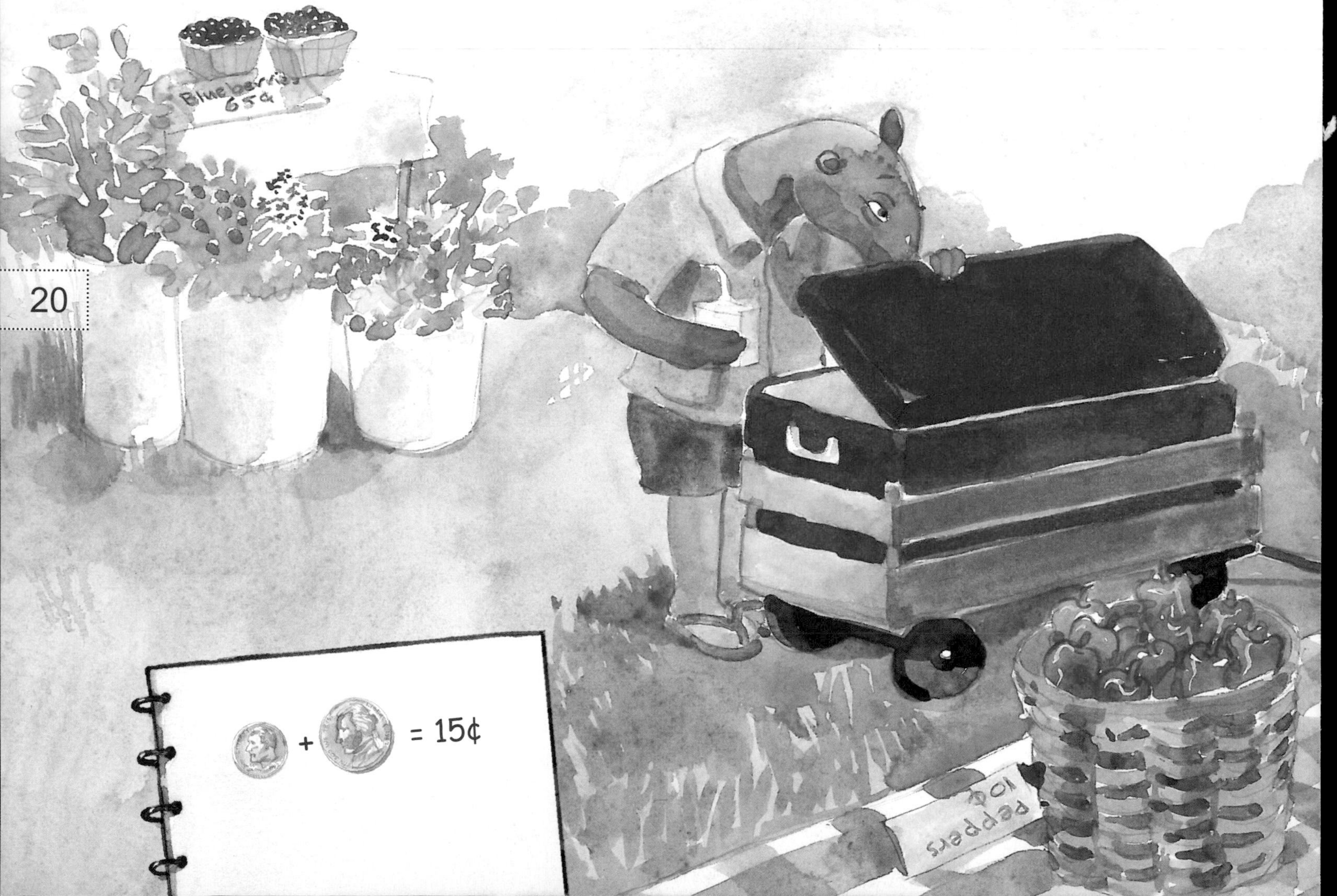

Blueberries
65¢

⊙ + ⊙ = 15¢

peppers
10¢

Wow! I found a dollar bill.

Bread 35¢

YARN 55¢

22

Enough Is Enough

Yum! Sebastian smells bread. A small loaf costs 35¢. Do they have enough money left?

Sebastian counts the rest of the coins. They have 60¢ left. And 60 is more than 35. "Yes! We can buy the bread!" Sebastian says. But Louie docs not hear him.

60¢ is more than 35¢.

Which Coins?

How will Sebastian pay the 35¢?

Sebastian picks two dimes, two nickels, and five pennies. He has 25 cents left. "We can save this for our next picnic," he says.

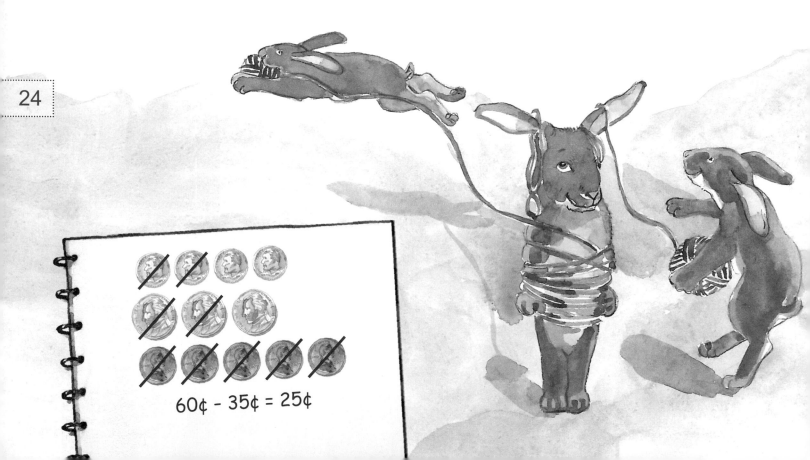

60¢ - 35¢ = 25¢

Louie's Lucky Day

Just then Sebastian sees something red go by. It's a flying disk! Sebastian picks it up.

"Where did you get this?" Sebastian asks.

"It's my lucky day!" Louie says. "I found a dollar. And guess how much this toy cost?"

$1.00 - $1.00 = $0

Let's Eat!

At last, it is time for the picnic. "We have everything we
need," Sebastian says. "Food, a toy ... and look! More friends!"

Now You Know

Look at the groups of coins below. Each group may add up to 20¢, 40¢, 50¢, or 75¢. Can you figure out how much each bunch of coins is worth?

1. = ?

2. = ?

3. = ?

4. = ?

5. = ?

ANSWERS:
1. 20¢
2. 40¢
3. 75¢
4. 40¢
5. 50¢

Words to Know

dollar—100 cents.
nickel—a coin worth five cents.
penny—a coin worth one cent.
quarter—a coin worth 25 cents.

Learn More

Books

Dalton, Julie. *Counting Money*. New York: Children's Press, 2005.

Pistoia, Sara. *Money*. Chanhassen, MN: Child's World, 2007.

Worth, Bonnie. *One Cent, Two Cents, Old Cent, New Cent: All About Money*. New York: Random House, 2008.

Web Sites

FunBrain
http://www.funbrain.com/brain/MathBrain/MathBrain.html

Math Circus
http://www.counton.org/games/circus

Index